I Can

Presented to

Kendyl

By

Mamaw Tammy

On

12/25/2020

Sit for a Bit book

I Can

written by **Kathryn O'Brien** *illustrated by* **Gillian Flint**

TYNDALE
K!DS

Tyndale House Publishers, Inc.
Carol Stream, Illinois

Visit Tyndale's website for kids at www.tyndale.com/kids.

TYNDALE is a registered trademark of Tyndale House Publishers, Inc. The Tyndale Kids logo is a trademark of Tyndale House Publishers, Inc.

I Can

Designed by Jacqueline L. Nuñez

Edited by Stephanie Rische

Published in association with the literary agency of D.C. Jacobson & Associates LLC, an Author Management Company. www.dcjacobson.com.

For manufacturing information regarding this product, please call 1-800-323-9400.

ISBN 978-1-4964-1117-4

Printed in China

22	21	20	19	18	17	16
7	6	5	4	3	2	1

A Note to Parents

Dear Parents,
As believers, we are called to know God's Word—to hide it and hold it in our hearts. What a wonderful opportunity and an awesome responsibility we have to share His Word, teach His life-changing promises, and impart His powerful truths to our children. My prayer is that God uses this book to help children learn, understand, and indeed hold God's Word in their little hearts for a lifetime.

—Kathryn O'Brien

The grass withers and the flowers fade,
but the word of our God stands forever.

Isaiah 40:8

I can

2

I can jump!

I can laugh!

I can run and play

and skip and dance.

I can sing and climb

and swim and swing!

I can.

5

I can do

I can do art.

I can do math.

I can do puzzles and puppet shows.

I can do cartwheels and karate.

I can do chores.

I can do kind deeds.

So many things to do!

9

I can do

everything

Everything?

Everything.

Nothing is too big or too

hard or too scary.

I can do
through Christ

14

everything

Christ.

That's a name for Jesus. The Messiah.

Our Savior. God's only Son.

He was born in a stable.

He died on a cross.

He rose from the dead.

And if you ask Him, He will forgive

your sins and live in your heart!

I can do
through Christ

everything
who

Who loves us,

protects us,

helps us,

saves us.

I can do
through Christ

everything
who gives

Gives grace.

Gives gifts.

Gives second chances.

Gives life.

I can do through Christ me.

everything
who gives

Me?

Me!

There's only one of me.

No one else is just like me.

Unique. Special. Wonderfully made. Me.

Even before I was born, He knew me!

I can do through Christ me

everything
who gives
strength.

Strength to try.

Strength to do my best.

Strength to believe that God will make a way.

He gives me strength!

I can do everything through Christ,
who gives me strength.

Philippians 4:13